Winnie the Pooh

ONE SPECIAL TREE

By K. Emily Hutta

Illustrated by
Carson Van Osten, John Kurtz
& the Disney Storybook Artists

One very hot, very dry day—in the middle of a summer that had been filled with hot, dry days—Winnie the Pooh had an idea. Actually, it was the same idea he'd had the afternoon before—and the afternoon before that.

"I think I'll go and sit in the shade of my favorite tree," Pooh said. "Yes." He nodded, agreeing wholeheartedly with himself. "That seems like a very good sort of thing for a bear to do on a day like today."

Now if a bear happened to doze off just a little when he was leaning against the trunk of his favorite tree, well, that was just the way it was with bears and favorite trees. Especially when the bear was drowsy from the heat and a rather-larger-than-usual midday meal.

And if that same bear happened to snore a little—or even quite a lot—his favorite tree could be counted on not to mind.

When Pooh woke up, it was some time later, and he was no longer leaning. He was lying on his back, staring straight up through the leaves to the sky.

Pooh was confused. Not because he had tipped over in his sleep—that happened all the time—but because the leaves on his favorite tree looked—well, there was really no polite way to put it—they looked very bad. They looked brownish and droopy instead of greenish and glossy.

It wasn't at all usual. It was, in fact, a mystery—and Pooh thought he might know just the rabbit to solve it.

Rabbit was carrying his watering can back and forth around his thirsty garden when Pooh arrived.

"I can't remember the last time it rained," Rabbit said to Pooh.

"You can't?" asked Pooh.

"No," said Rabbit. "Can you?"

"Well, no," said Pooh. "But that's not why I'm here."

"Oh, you have a reason for being here?" asked Rabbit.

Pooh had to think quite hard for a moment, but then he remembered.

"I'm here because I'm worried about my favorite tree."

Rabbit went to look at the tree with Pooh.

Rabbit walked around the trunk several times, muttering to himself. Then he backed up and squinted at the tree from a distance. Finally, at Pooh's suggestion, Rabbit stretched out on his back and gazed up at the leaves.

Pooh waited patiently—and just when it appeared that a bear might doze off for a second time in a single afternoon—Rabbit spoke.

"This tree looks just the way my vegetables look when they don't get enough water," Rabbit said.

"Oh! Perhaps we could give it some water," Pooh suggested.

"Yes," said Rabbit, looking at his watering can and then looking at the enormous tree. "But I think we're going to need help."

Pooh and Rabbit set out to find more friends to help them help Pooh's favorite tree. They stopped at Owl's house first.

"I know just the tree you're talking about," Owl said. "I like to sit in the tip-top branches of that very tree and watch the sun rise over the Hundred-Acre Wood. It's a particularly fine place to think about the bigness and smallness of things.

"If the tree with the glorious view needs our assistance," Owl said, rummaging around in his closet to find a bucket. "And if that tree also happens to be our favorite bear's favorite tree—well, therefore and also heretofore and possibly subsequent to that, I would be honored to do whatever I can to help."

Pooh, Rabbit, and Owl went together to Piglet's house. Piglet was in the middle of something when they arrived. However, when he heard about the tree, he dropped everything—which resulted in a great deal of flour settling in places that it wasn't really meant to be.

"I'll worry about this mess later," Piglet said, starting to pull empty pitchers from the shelf.

"That tree is where I collect the biggest and most delicious haycorns every year," Piglet said. "It has given me so much. The least I can do is try to give something back."

Rabbit looked thoughtful. "That tree has given me a lot, too," he said. "It's given me bendy twigs to make baskets for my vegetables in the spring. And nice dry twigs to make fires in the winter."

"If you want to bring all of those pitchers, Piglet," Rabbit said, "we can help you carry them."

So Rabbit carried two of Piglet's pitchers, and Pooh offered to carry Rabbit's watering can—and the friends were soon on their way.

They hadn't gone very far when there was a sudden commotion.

It all seemed to start with Tigger, who bounded into Rabbit, who bumped into Pooh, who tripped Piglet, who landed in Owl's bucket. Luckily, when they all sorted themselves out, nothing—and no one—was broken.

"Why are you hurling pitchers around, Long Ears?" Tigger asked.

Rabbit made a peculiar growling sound.

Piglet explained that they were on their way to water the tree with the best haycorns and bendiest branches.

"Hoo-hoo-hoo! I'll come, too!" Tigger said. "Helping is what tiggers do best!"

Kanga was outside hanging laundry when her friends came by to ask for help. Kanga didn't hesitate for a moment.

"Come, Roo!" Kanga called. "We have something important to do!"

"What?" Roo asked excitedly. "What are we going to do?"

"You hold one handle of the laundry tub, and I'll hold the other," Kanga said. "I'll explain on the way."

"Oh, look!" Roo shouted a short while later. "There's my swinging tree! That's where I learned to swing!"

"I used to bring him to this tree when he was just a wee Roo," Kanga said. "The branches are so sturdy and strong. I trusted this tree—this good, reliable tree—to protect my wild boy, and it always did.

"Now we have the opportunity to return the favor," Kanga said, hugging a slightly embarrassed Roo.

"So this is the tree every-buddy's been talking about?" Tigger asked. "Why didn't any-buddy say so?

"I happen to know all about this tree," Tigger said. "For exampling, I know that it has the crunchiest leaves in the whole Hundred-Acre Wood!"

"How do you know that?" Roo asked.

"Because last fall, I tried them all!" Tigger said.

"First, I jumped in the leaf piles near Rabbit's garden. . . ."

"That was you?" Rabbit sputtered. "I spent days raking those leaves!"

"Thanks, Long Ears," said Tigger, "for going to all that trouble just for me! But after jumping in all the leaves from all the trees in the Hundred-Acre Wood, I can say with authorinity—artherninny—attoruni—well, I can say for sure that the leaves from this tree were the crunchiest of all!"

Just then, Eeyore arrived.

Roo gasped.

Pooh gulped.

"Eeyore!" Piglet said breathlessly. "You seem to . . . That is, did you know . . . Are you at all aware that . . . ?"

"You have a tree growing out of your back," Pooh said.

Eeyore looked over his shoulder. "It's not growing there. I'm just giving it a ride."

"I thought I would plant it here," Eeyore said, pointing to a sunny spot. "Next to the sweet-smelling blossom tree. Every spring this tree is covered with blossoms," Eeyore said. "It always makes me feel, well, nearly cheerful. When I saw that the tree looked sad, I wanted to cheer it up. So I brought a little tree to keep it company."

"Everyone feels better when they have a little company," Pooh said.

Then Eeyore's friends—all of them together—helped him plant the little tree.

"Now," Rabbit said firmly, dusting off his hands, "it's time to water."

"Everyone!" he called. "Fill your buckets and pitchers and etceteras in the stream and carry them to the tree!"

Tigger borrowed one of Piglet's pitchers, filled it to the brim, and spilled all of it when he took his first bounce. Pooh tripped on a tree root and soaked himself from head to foot. Roo fell into the stream trying to pull a full laundry tub onto the bank.

"I have an idea," Kanga said as she fished Roo out of the stream. "Why don't we all do what we do best?"

"Eeyore is quite strong, so he can pull the full containers out of the stream," she suggested. Eeyore squared his shoulders proudly.

"The rest of us can form a line from the stream to the trees and pass the water from one to the other," Kanga said. "Tigger and Roo can be last. When they get the water, they can bounce to spread it around under the trees."

So on that day—and every hot, dry day from then on—the friends all came together and watered the very special tree (which was an easier name to remember than Pooh's-favorite–Roo's-swinging–Eeyore's-sweet-smelling–Owl's-glorious-viewing–Piglet's-best-haycorning–Rabbit's-bendiest-branches–Tigger's-crunchiest-leaves tree).

The very special tree soon began to look green and splendid again. The friends also watered the little keep-you-company tree—which grew taller and stronger every day.

Then one day, something changed—and that something was the weather. The sky turned from blue to gray, and the wind began to blow.

"You're splashing us again, Tigger," Rabbit complained.

"I think the sky is splashing us," Pooh said, looking up just in time for a big, round raindrop to land on his nose.

The friends ran to the very special tree. They stood together under the tree's big, sheltering branches—and they cheered—for the rain and the trees and each other.

The next sunny afternoon, when Pooh came to sit in the shade of his favorite tree, he found Roo resting under the keep-you-company tree.

"Someday this tree will be big enough for all of us to sit under," Roo said. "But for now, it's just the right size for me."

Roo stayed for a while and talked to Pooh about this and that—and then he hopped off to find something more lively to do.

Pooh settled back against his favorite tree. Above him, in the branches, birds snuggled in their nests. Shy little animals peeked out from the safety of knotholes in the sturdy trunk. Bees buzzed about their business in a well-hidden hive. Winnie the Pooh started to snore softly.

All was well in the Hundred-Acre Wood.

Trees

Next time you're near a very special tree,
Take a moment to think about generosity.
Trees give us food, shelter, shade, and a view;
Since they take care of us, we should take care of
them, too.

Thank You, Trees

Thank you, trees,
For cooling shade
And lemons to
Make lemonade.

For pretty buds
And dappled light
And autumn leaves
That drift in flight.

For sturdy limbs
Where we can play
Or sit and dream
The day away.

Nature Activity

"One Special Tree" tells the story of a tree in the Hundred-Acre Wood that is special to Pooh and his friends for many different reasons. Pooh likes to sit in the shade of the tree and snooze. Owl likes to sit high up in its branches and enjoy the view. Piglet uses its haycorns to make his delicious muffins, and Rabbit uses the twigs to make baskets. Tigger loves to jump in the tree's crunchy leaves in the fall, and Eeyore loves to smell its sweet-smelling blossoms in the spring.

When the friends realize that the very special tree needs their help to stay healthy and strong, they all work together to take care of the tree that has given so much to them. Next time you're outside, take a close look at the trees around you. What's special about them? Do they keep your house from getting too hot in the summer? Do they grow fruit that you can eat? Do they provide shelter for birds and animals? Are they a glorious place to sit and dream?

Maybe you can help take care of a tree that lives near you. You can even plant a new tree, the way Eeyore did. Ask a grown-up if there's a good place in your yard or a local park to plant a tree. It might need some help from you to grow, but it will return your generosity with gifts that only a tree can give!

At Kohl's, we believe the simple act of caring creates a sense of community. Thanks to people like you, over the past 10 years Kohl's Cares for Kids ® has raised millions of dollars to support children in the communities we serve. Throughout the year, Kohl's sells special Kohl's Cares for Kids merchandise with 100% of the net profit benefiting children's health and education initiatives nationwide.

Kohl's Cares for Kids is our way of supporting our customers and improving children's lives. So when you turn the pages of this book, remember you're not only reading a fun-filled adventure, you're also helping make a difference in the life of a child.

For more information about Kohl's Cares for Kids programs, visit www.kohlscorporation.com.

SUSTAINABLE
FORESTRY
INITIATIVE

Certified Fiber
Sourcing

www.sfiprogram.org

PWC-SFICOC-260
FOR TEXT PAPER ONLY

For more Disney Press fun, visit www.disneybooks.com